HOW TO BE A SUCCESS:

A GUIDE

FOR YOUNG

PEOPLE

Zimmie Williams

Sergeant, Los Angeles Police Department (Ret.),
Former Member of the United States Navy

How To Be A Success: A Guide For Young People
©2021, Zimmie Williams

ISBN: 978-1-09836-940-8
ISBN eBook: 978-1-09836-941-5

CONTENTS

CHAPTER 1:

THE INTRODUCTION:

Why do some people fail in life? Why do some (after leaving their teen years, and venturing into adulthood) fail to succeed?

A simple answer could be that they simply were not given the tools they needed to succeed earlier in life. They were not equipped for the journey they would find themselves on as they left behind their youthful beginnings.

The purpose of this book is to provide a road map, a guide – a helping hand.

CHAPTER 2:

MY OWN JOURNEY.

According to most statistical information, I should not have become a success – of any measure. I was born to a single mother, in Chicago, Illinois, at Cook County Hospital, in the year 1959. I was a survivor of a bad divorce at age ten - when the man who became my step-father (my father), a battle-hardened Combat Veteran of the Korean War, and my mother went their separate ways. After my parent's divorce, I lacked strong male leadership and role modeling in my young life. Due to my shyness and wholehearted interest in academic achievement in school, I suffered through school bullying in the early years of my education.

After the marriage ended, my mother, and my brothers and I were thrust into a world of "just getting by." We didn't live in the best neighborhoods. We didn't attend the best schools. We didn't associate with the best people.

But there was a silver lining to what could have otherwise been a not so happy ending.

My ultimate success in life came by the way of "strong mentors."

Good, caring teachers. Strong support staff in the schools I attended as a youth. Kindness, generosity on the part of the adults who ventured in and out of my life, along with my willingness as a young person to be guided by them.

CHAPTER 3:

MENTORS

Young people need strong mentors. In fact, the stronger the better. The harder, tougher, and more demanding the better.

In my own life, it was the mentors who pushed me, demanded of me, challenged me. They were the people I learned from, and eventually learned to respect and emulate the most.

My stepfather, Sergeant Clarence Williams, was a "tank commander" in the United States Army Tanker Corps. He, and all the thousands of young men like him, left the safety, security and sanctity of their homes to board warships that would carry them to their ultimate combat objective - Korea.

The Korean War began June 25th, 1950, and lasted until July 2nd, 1953. It cost the lives of 33,686 Americans. My stepfather did not lose his life in the Korean War, but he (and the thousands of young men like him) did shed blood there.

He was wounded seriously twice; once when he and his crew dismounted from the safety of their multi-ton tank to engage the enemy on foot. During the dismount, he was shot by a Korean soldier, with a rifle. The bullet was handed to him when he awoke from surgery in an Army Field Hospital.

Another serious injury he incurred during the war was a burn mark on his scalp. The burn mark injury resulted when a super-heated anti-tank round scraped against his head during combat operations against the Korean Army.

My stepfather was a hard man, he was a tough man. After each of his combat related injuries, he returned to command his tank, to lead his men in battle.

My stepfather was a great combat leader. He took care of and protected his men. He, as a soldier, followed orders, and led from the front.

When he took command of my young life, at the age of two-years-old, he continued to provide strong leadership.

My stepfather taught me how to be a man. How to carry myself as a man. How to provide for my family as a man. How to manage and run my household, like a man.

I was only "under his command" for eight years of my life, but his strength, his courage, his valor, and his family leadership style has remained with me for my entire life.

My stepfather taught me that a "strong man" a "good man" always has a job. He brings his pay check home to his wife. A strong man ensures that his family always has a secure place in life. A strong man always ensures that the "bills are paid," and the refrigerator is always "full."

One of the things I will always remember and cherish about my stepfather is that each year at Christmas, there was literally no space beneath the Christmas tree that wasn't covered by presents. The refrigerator was never without food.

My stepfather taught me "how to be a man." A STRONG MAN.

I wrote about the influence my stepfather had on my life in an effort to illustrate the value, the necessity, and the absolute need for strong mentors in a child's life.

Without his strong influence in the earliest chapters of my life, I don't know what might have become of me.

After the divorce of my parents, I found mentors in the schools I attended. The teachers who challenged me to always do better, to think deeper, to strive harder. It was the teachers who were the most demanding, the most unforgiving of intellectual laziness that I now have the fondest memories of.

CHAPTER 4:

BECOMING AN ADULT

The step into adulthood can sometimes be the hardest to take. When we step into adulthood, we leave behind the sometimes carefree life of letting others lead, guide, direct, and make "adult decisions" for us.

When we "step into adulthood" we become the "captain of our own ship."

When we become an adult, it is no longer the fault or responsibility of our parents or grandparents if our laundry is not done. We become responsible if the house is not clean, if the bills are not paid, if the refrigerator is empty. We become responsible for renewing our driver's license when it is due, paying the car insurance, vehicle registration, vehicle maintenance, and upkeep.

We become responsible to set the alarm clock to ensure we awake in time to prepare for work.

I took my own step into adulthood at the age of 17 and a half, during my senior year at Lakewood High School, located in the city of Lakewood, California, in the year 1977.

In 1975, I enrolled in Lakewood High School as a Junior. Upon enrollment, I made a decision pertaining to "elective" class selection that would alter, shape, and change the rest of my life. I opted to select a class listed as Junior Navy R.O.T.C. (Recruit Officers Training Corp).

This class selection was vital to my ultimate future enrichment and development as a young person due to the instructors leading the class. Commander Johnson, and Chief Diaz. Both of these men were retired United States Navy veterans. These men took an interest in me, a poor kid, from a broken home, who because of my parent's divorce, was reduced to using "lunch tickets" (welfare) in the cafeteria of a school located in a very prosperous city.

One day, in the middle of my third year of Lakewood, I was summoned to the office of the Commander. He and Chief Diaz then closed the door. As a 17-year-old student, I couldn't help but to think silently to myself, "what have I done now?" The two military men gently began to probe. The commander asked, "what do you plan to do after High School son?" Taking a moment to process the question, I responded "I really don't know sir." Having been brought up in a blue-collar family, the prospect of going to college had never occurred to me. I would have most probably applied for a job at a local hamburger stand. The commander asked, "have you ever thought of joining the Navy?" These men were proposing something that I had never given a second's thought to.

After I left school that day, I thought about it, I thought about it a lot. I thought about my stepfather, what he had done and endured in service to our country, during the Korean War. I respected my stepfather (my first major mentor) and I loved him. I knew that volunteering for service to our country would make him proud. A few days later, I stepped back into Commander Johnson's office. I was 17 and a half years old. A few weeks later, I became the newest recruit member of the United States Navy.

BOOT CAMP:

I won't bore the reader with all the nuances of military training in boot camp. I will let it suffice to say that boot camp is HARD. A few of the 100 men who were assigned to our recruit training company could not handle the physical, emotional, and psychological strain that we were put under in our efforts to become United States Navy sailors. Those who were unable to adapt to the life of military service "washed-out," and were removed from training.

With these things being said, the actual point of this part of the book is to talk about the Drill Instructors. Like Drill Instructors in every training facility, in every service, in every military across the globe, these men and women are both feared and revered. They were feared because during the eight weeks it took to survive Navy boot camp, they had absolute power over our young lives. Punishment was meted out daily; any deviation from orders, directives, or instructions were corrected immediately.

While in training, during boot camp, the trainee comes to loath these dedicated men and women, because of the physical and psychological transformations they force our young minds and bodies to endure – sometimes you even start to hate them.

But after training, after we have been transformed from ordinary civilians into marines, soldiers, airmen, and sailors, we come to love them for what they gave us.

For many of us, especially those like me, those without fathers in the home, those lacking strong male or female role models, these once feared instructors are remembered in an almost fatherly and motherly way. I can honestly say now, many years down the road into manhood, that I love my Drill Instructors. I always will.

MY HELICOPTER SQUADRON IN HAWII:

After graduation from boot camp and attending technical specialty school, I was assigned to a helicopter squadron in Barbers Point, Hawaii.

As a still 18-year-old sailor, the Navy was a whole new experience for me. I was living on an island, in the Pacific Ocean, with a few thousand other young sailors sent there by the United States Government. In Hawaii, we were the United States Navy.

The most import aspect of my time in Hawaii, assigned to a Helicopter Squadron, is that while there, and then for six months aboard a Navy Warship, I was under the total and absolute control of sailors and "commissioned officers" who guided and directed every aspect of my life.

While under the command of these men (there were no senior female commissioned officers or senior petty officers stationed there at the time), I was becoming a man. I was slowly but surely leaving childhood behind.

After leaving the Navy in the year 1980, I was lost. When my enlistment ended, so did my connection to these strong, stable, reliable, dependable, quality men. I was on my own.

What I was unaware of as a still 21-year-old military "veteran," is that my mind had made a virtual exact copy of these men. A copy that I would carry with me for the rest of my life.

When I entered the Los Angeles Police Academy in 1981, at the age of 21, there were more "mentors" waiting for me in that institution. Strong men and women, of good moral character. While in the Police Academy, I would learn many things about police work. I would learn many things about character. I would add these things to what the United States Navy had given to me.

As the years passed, and my career progressed form basic officer, to training officer, to senior lead officer, and then police sergeant, I found myself always reaching back into the "bag of tricks" regarding manhood I had picked up along the way in my journey.

As a street police officer, I protected the citizens I was responsible for in the patrol sectors to which I was assigned, the way my stepfather had protected me, as a child. As a police sergeant, I used my rank as a "supervisor" to protect the officers I had been given responsibility for.

ANALYSIS:

I included my own life experiences under the stewardship and direction of my war-hardened, combat tested stepfather, the teachers in the schools I attended, the Drill Instructors in boot camp, the officers and chief petty officers I served under in the Navy, the instructors at the Police Academy, and all the other "mentors" in my life because I want the young reader of this book to take a look around you. I want you to take a second look at your father, mother, your stepfather, your grandfather, grandmother, your uncle, your science teacher, gym coach, track coach, your social studies teacher, the guidance counselor, the assistant principle, the school principle, and all the strong and caring people in your life; I want you to appreciate them, to seek to understand them, to emulate them, to learn from them. Why? Because these people, who are with and around you right now, at this very moment in time in your life are YOUR FUTURE.

CHAPTER 5:

DEVELOP A VISION FOR YOUR FUTURE.

Why is it so important to "Develop A Plan For Your Future?"

Because without developing a "plan for your future," it's like trying to construct a 50-story building without a building design.

A "plan for your future" is a blue print, a road map, a guide, a direction finder, coordinates to an objective.

No military engagement, structural building project, or major event can be successful without developing a "plan."

By planning for your future, you a taking the "long-view" of your life. You are looking beyond your present position.

By the 9th or 10th grade, in High School, a young person should already have begun the process of "looking towards their future."

Why? Why is it important to "look towards your future?"

Here is why: Imagine that you have decided to sail to Europe from America. However, because you never sat down and "developed a plan" you simply go to the edge of the sea, board a sail boat, and cast-off.

PROBLEMS:

1. You never took sailing lessons. You have no clue as to how to operate or guide a sail boat.

2. You never took the time to look at a world map. You have no idea where Europe is located.

3. You don't know how to navigate. Because of your inability to navigate, you are at the mercy of the ocean.

4. You never stocked the sail boat with provisions. As a result, once you get lost at sea, you will most probably perish due to lack of food.

5. You took no communications system aboard the sail boat with you. So, once you have become lost in the vastness of the ocean, you will have no ability to call for help or rescue.

This analogy of failing to plan for an ocean voyage from America to Europe is the same thing that happens when we leave childhood and venture into adulthood without a "plan for the future." You are lost.

So, how do you as a teenager begin to develop a plan for your future? It's simple. You spend time with your MENTORS. You talk to them. You question them. You learn from them. You EMULATE them. You COPY them.

A Vision For Your Future should include most (or all) of the following:

1. What college you will attend after graduating High School.

2. What courses you plan to take while in college.

3. What career path you plan to follow.

4. What type of business you would be interested in starting once you leave school.

5. What type of marriage partner would be suitable for your chosen path in life. WARNING: Avoid those who could pull you "off course" of your life plan.

6. Where you would like to live.

7. Investing in the purchase of a home, condo, or townhouse.

8. Looking towards the future college education of your children. NOTE: As you look forward towards the future education of your children, you must establish a method of paying for their college, or assisting them.

9. Looking forward to your (inevitable) retirement, and developing a strong financial plan for it.

CHAPTER 6:

EMULATE AND MODEL PEOPLE YOU ADMIRE AND RESPECT.

Why is modeling and emulating (copying) the behavior and traits of those we admire and respect so important? It's because these are the people who have already "walked the trail," have "won the battle," have "climbed the mountain." These are the people who can "show you the way."

Young people are in just the beginning stages of their lives. Looking to and modeling people with good moral character, with strong convictions and integrity, people who are honest, straightforward, and trustworthy, is one of the best ways to find your way to your own path of future success.

This is why it is so important for young people to have good, strong, well intentioned role models and mentors.

CHAPTER 7:

LEARN SOMETHING NEW EVERY DAY.

Why is it important to "learn something new every day?" It's because the human mind is a complex system of neurological material. The mind was designed to be challenged, developed, stretched, and advanced.

By learning something new every single day, we increase electrical conductivity between the 80 billion or so neurons that make up the human brain. This "new" electrical conductivity is "knowledge."

The things that we have knowledge of and already know how to do, are already a part of us. We already own them. When we push ourselves to acquire new knowledge, a new skill, a new language, a new system, a new source of information, we are expanding our intellectual abilities. We are making ourselves better, stronger, and more capable people.

CHAPTER 8:

READ SOMETHING EVERY DAY.

I have read a number of business success articles which chronicled how most billionaires read something new every day. Every single day.

Why? Why are people who are already fabulously wealthy "investing" their time in reading "something new" every day? It's because they are expanding their knowledge base. They are broadening the reach of their (already brilliant) minds.

When I was in school, I never (ever) read for pleasure. It wasn't until I left High School and entered the Navy that I began to grasp the true value in reading. The commissioned officers and chief petty officers who had absolute power and control over the sailors under their command were all avid readers. Why? Knowledge of "new information." By reading, we leave our current level of education and experience and venture into a whole new one. Knowledge is power.

By reading, we can (while sitting in a chair), leave our homes or apartments, or even a Navy Warship at sea, and travel to foreign countries, meet new and interesting people, and experience things that had been previously unknown to us. By reading, we broaden our minds, expand our knowledge, increase our understanding of things we are uncertain of, and gain knowledge of things that had been totally alien to us prior to picking up a book, and engaging our ravenous brain cells.

By reading, we can experience the brilliance of some of the greatest minds that have ever lived throughout history: Astronauts, theologians, playwrights, historians, world and space travelers.

By reading, we are engaging in an ever-increasing expansion of our basic vocabularies.

You should read something new every single day of your life!

CHAPTER 9:

DIVERSIFY YOUR SKILL LEVEL

What exactly does this mean? Diversify? Diversification means to "expand your abilities."

In the modern world, when companies are sold off to new owners, employees are "let go," companies "go out of business," the business needs of the company may change to meet the new technological needs of ever evolving industry standards. By "diversifying" your skill level, if you are suddenly thrust back into the job market, and are faced with looking for brand new employment, a well-diversified skill level portfolio will be much more attractive to a future employer than one which shows "limited skill range."

So, if you already have a skill-set in computers, then reach outside your current abilities and learn about the information and communication systems that will most assuredly dominate the future of world technologies.

If you are already a bus driver, learn how to be a truck driver. If you are interested in truly expanding your mind, learn a second language, and possibly even a third. Think of how impressed future dates will be when you take them to a new restaurant and you order the meal in Italian, or Spanish, or German.

Knowledge of a second language will most certainly impress employers during future job interviews.

By diversifying our skill-level, we can not only increase our attractiveness to future employers, but also develop self-confidence. A self-confidence that even if a company closes down due to a changing market of societal needs, you have mastered yourself, and evolved into a human who can "improvise, adapt, and overcome" any adversity they are faced with.

CHAPTER 10:

INVEST IN YOURSELF.

What does it mean to "invest in yourself?"

To invest in yourself means that you have engaged in a determined effort to develop and enrich yourself.

By investing in yourself, you build up and develop your personal abilities, skill level, experience and character.

So, how does a "younger person" invest in themselves?

A young person "invests in themselves" by listening to the teachers in the schools they attend while in the rigidly structured environments of the educational systems. A young person invests in themselves by turning away from gangs, and drugs, and people (peers) who are going nowhere but DOWN.

A young person invests in themselves by spending time with QUALITY PEOPLE: People, mentors, and peers who will enrich them, encourage them, challenge them.

A young person invests in themselves by paying attention to the teacher while in science class, health class, social studies class, history class, home economics class, automotive repair class, French and Spanish language studies class, and physical education classes.

A young person invests in themselves by spending quality time with their parents, uncles, aunts and grand-parents, and asking them, if they were 16, 17, 18, or 19 or 20, what would they "do differently" in their lives, if they had it to do all over again, then make a concerted effort learn from their mistakes.

Invest in yourself.

CHAPTER 11:

ESTABLISH "CORE VALUES"

What are "Core Values?"

Core Values are things such as:

- Honesty

- Integrity

- Truthfulness

- Loyalty

- Devotion to family and friends

- Self-Respect

and,

And, an unwillingness to associate with people who lack the vast majority of these qualities. These are people who do not find value in your Core Beliefs (your Core Values).

By developing a set of "Core Values" for your life that you are unwilling to violate (under any circumstance), you are developing a set of "Character Traits" that cannot be compromised......by anyone!

CHAPTER 12:

STEP OUT OF YOUR COMFORT ZONE

What does it mean to "Step Outside of Your Comfort Zone?"

Stepping outside of your comfort zone means that you are willing to engage in (productive) activities that are character enriching. NOTE: Things that you would not normally do.

How this applies to "you," the young person, is like this:

If your favorite activity is playing basketball, then learn to ski.

If surfing is your sport, then learn to play tennis.

If computers give you your thrill, then take a shooting course at a gun range.

If your English is flawless, then learn to speak German, and then make plans to one day visit Germany, so that you may practice your new language craft.

If all your friends are "nerds" and 'geeks" (like me), I want you to make friends with people who ride motorcycles, and jet skis; people who on a whim will suddenly plan a trip to the beach, or Hawaii, or London England.

I want you to make friends with people who will challenge you, people who will spur intellectual growth and diversity, character strength and maturity.

Diversify yourself.

CHAPTER 13:

ATTEND COLLEGE (IF YOU ARE ABLE) EDUCATE YOURSELF

Why should a young person attend college or university? Because that is where smart people go to become even smarter, or even more brilliant. Or not so smart people (like me), go to become smarter.

In the modern age of cyber space and computer technologies, a person who has not acquired at least a minimal amount of technical knowledge and advancement is like a person in the 1800's, someone who is only rudimentarily equipped to function in a modern society.

In college, you will be exposed to the brilliant minds of teachers, professors, and other academia.

In college, you will be made aware of both your intellectual strengths, and your weaknesses.

Colleges are where (most) of our civic, military, and political leaders have been molded, shaped, and sharpened by the minds of intellectual titans.

If you do elect to attend college, and graduate with an associate's degree, bachelor's degree, master's degree or PhD, you will have a "calling card" of demonstrated intellectual achievement that will follow you and open doors for the rest of your life.

If you can, go to college.

CHAPTER 14:

TRADE SCHOOLS AND INTERNSHIPS

TRADE SCHOOLS:

Trade schools teach things like auto repair, welding, carpentry, dental assisting, secretarial skills, and other "trades" that can be relatively more easily acquired without the need to attend a four-year college or university.

INTERNSHIPS:

Internships are "jobs" that are done "without financial compensation." In other words, "you don't get paid."

Why would a young person embark upon undertaking an "Internship?"

Internships are a way for a young person to "get their foot in the door." It is a way for a company, corporation, law firm, dental office, car dealership, or other entity of interest to "take a look at you" as a potential "new hire."

By undertaking an internship, you get to "present yourself to the company."

You are afforded an opportunity to demonstrate your reliability, trust-worthiness, dependability, honesty, and professionalism.

Many professional companies use "internships" as a "screening process" for persons they are interested in hiring.

PROFESSIONAL ADMONITION:

If you are fortunate enough to be granted an internship with a major company, law firm, or other professional organization. There are a few simple rules you must adhere to ensure success:

1. Always be on time. In fact, always be half and hour to an hour early – every single work day.

2. Always dress in a professional manner. Business or other industry appropriate attire.

3. Learn your assigned duties or job quickly. By demonstrating that you are a "quick learner" you prove yourself as a reliable and capable asset to the company or organization.

4. Work harder than those around you. Make yourself "needed."

5. Keep your mouth shut. Do not engage in company politics or create adversarial alliances when you are not yet "a part of the team."

6. Do what you are told. You are "not the boss." They are!

7. Be grateful. Even though you are not getting paid, demonstrate gratuity for the opportunity.

8. And finally, ALWAYS BE PROFESSIOANL!

CHAPTER 15:

MAINTAIN PHYSICAL FITNESS

Why is maintaining a fit, healthy body important for the young person?

A number of scientific and medical studies have repeatedly demonstrated that those who maintain even a moderate level of good physical fitness suffer from less health problems, as compared to those who do not.

By maintaining a good physical fitness program, you not only keep "your machine" (your physical body) in great shape, but studies have also demonstrated that the mind derives many benefits from a regular exercise program as well. Physical fitness and a strong athletic routine have also been proven to increase intelligence.

It is recommended by a number of studies related to physical fitness that the human body receives many benefits from some form of exercise for just 30 minute each day.

By maintaining a strong, fit, athletic body, not only are you contributing to your overall health, you (as a young person) also affect your outer appearance – the exterior of your body.

As sad as it is, humans are judged by our appearance; those who are thought to be more attractive sometimes are ushered to the front of the line, while those who viewed as less attractive are sometimes ushered to the rear.

We have no control of our genetic makeup, we received our genes from our parents, grandparents, and great grandparents. We do, however have control over the foods we eat, and the decision to exercise - or not.

While in both United Sates Navy boot camp, and the Los Angeles Police Academy, as both a young sailor (I enlisted before my 18th birthday), and a young Los Angeles Police Department recruit, we did a lot of physical exercise. A lot of running, pushups, jumping jacks, pullups, sit-ups, and other "grass-drills." This physical exertion every day produced young men and women with superbly fit and healthy bodies.

You must take care of your body – it is the only one you will ever have in this life.

So, what constitutes "exercise?"

- Walking

- Running

- Swimming

- Lifting weights

- Cycling

- Jogging

- Martial Arts

- Boxing

- Yoga

- Pilates

- Walking the dog

- Gardening

- Housework

- Dancing

- Surfing

- Skiing

- Hiking

- Wrestling

- Mountain climbing

Do Something!

CHAPTER 16:

EAT HEALTHY FOODS

What are "healthy foods?"

Healthy foods are those that are well balanced in nutritional values. They contain protein, fiber, fat, and all the vitamins and minerals necessary to maintain our bodies as designed.

What are considered "unhealthy" foods? Those that don't contribute to your overall good health and fitness.

I think it would be safe to say that it is "unhealthy" for a person to consume (alone) an entire extra-large pizza every single day, while getting absolutely zero physical exercise.

It is "unhealthy" to consume an entire chocolate cake all by yourself (every day). Or whatever sugar and fat laden food product that over-burdens your body with useless calories that it cannot burn.

Be smart, listen to what the teachers (mentors) teach you in Health and Fitness class while in school.

Be fit and healthy!

CHAPTER 17:

BE FINANCIALLY RESPONSIBLE

Your personal finances are what allow you to live the type of life you desire. If your personal finances are in disarray, there is a pretty good chance that your life will be too.

As a teenager, it is most likely that your personal finances are under the control of your parents. This is fine; however, just because you are "managing" limited funds given to you as a "weekly allowance" does not mean it is too early in your life to begin thinking about proper money management. The financial habits you develop early in life (your teen years) are setting the stage for how you manage your money later on in life. If as soon as you receive your allowance, you rush to the store and spend the entire amount on either new video games, new phone accessories, clothing, or other items, without putting even a portion of it away for a "rainy day," you are setting up a pattern of being a "spendthrift." A person who cannot manage money.

A spendthrift personality is one that as soon as they are handed $20 in allowance, it is spent within an hour (or less) of receipt. If this negative habit is not broken, and carried into adulthood, this will be the person who spends his or her entire paycheck within hours or just a few days after receiving it from their employer.

As a young person, you should engage in a conscious effort to save (put away) at least 10% of any monies put under your control. Whether the funds are a result of allowance given by parents, payment for babysitting, mowing or raking lawns, or washing cars. A portion of any income must be saved for the future.

By doing this in your "teen years," you are establishing sound financial practices that will (hopefully) stay with you for the remainder of your life.

CREDIT CARDS:

If your parents provided you with your own credit card, this will be the beginning of your experience in "managing credit."

If your parents did not provide financial guidance when you were given the card, then "I" will provide it here.

Your personal credit rating is EXTREMELY IMPORTANT!

In our modern society, a person's credit rating (good, or bad) speaks for you in your absence (by way of background checks, and financial loan offers from potential creditors). Having a "good credit rating" is a very positive thing, while having a "bad credit rating" can be an EXTREMELY NEGATIVE thing.

By maintaining a "good credit rating," you can obtain a low interest auto loan, bank loan, buy a home or townhouse, or condo, and finance other financial interests.

By having a "bad credit rating," life becomes much more difficult. A bad credit rating may mean that requests for loans from banks and other financial intuitions are DENIED. Car loans are harder to get. Renting an apartment becomes more difficult. Buying a home nearly impossible.

Many professional organizations view persons with "poor" or "bad" credit ratings as undesirable for hiring.

Another negative aspect of irresponsible spending is if once you obtain a credit card in your name, you utilize more than 30% of the "available" credit balance on the card, your credit rating will be lowered, SUBSTANTIALLY.

Spend time talking about credit and finances with your parents, grandparents, or teachers.

Be financially smart!

CHAPTER 18:

DEVELOP GOOD RELATIONSHIPS (AVOID BAD PEOPLE)

What are "good relationships?"

A "good relationship" is one that has a positive influence on your life.

A "bad relationship" is one that brings negative influences into your life.

How do we know if a person in our life is "good" or "bad" for us? By what they bring into our lives.

If a person (a peer, friend, or family member) chooses to be law abiding, upstanding, loyal, faithful and honest to us, and those around them, this is a "good influence"

If a person (a peer, friend, or family member) chooses to step outside the law (to engage in criminal behavior), this is not a good influence in our lives.

People who use illegal drugs, commit thefts at retail stores, consume alcoholic beverages and operate a motor vehicle upon the roadway are generally not considered a person of "good moral character."

Persons of "poor moral character" must be avoided at all costs.

Be smart. Don't associate with BAD PEOPLE.

CHAPTER 19:

AVOID "ADDICTIONS"

Why do "young people" (sometimes) develop addictions?

I think for three basic reasons:

1. Peer pressure.

2. Boredom.

3. Trying to escape physical, psycological, or emotional pain.

PEER PRESSURE: As a teenager (many years ago) I too felt the effects of "negative" peer pressure. The pressure to "conform." The pressure to "be liked." The pressure to "be accepted" as a member of the group.

As teenagers are moving in the biological direction of becoming an adult, they are searching for where they fit-in with certain peer groups. They are searching for - and hoping for - acceptance. Sometimes, if they are affected by issues such as "low self-esteem," or parental abuse or neglect in the home, they may feel they are not worthy of true love and respect by peer members on the "upper-track" (the 'high achievers'). Instead, they will gravitate towards those on the lower end of the acceptance scale. Sometimes, those on the lower end of the scale, may not embody the most desirable character traits. These persons partake in the utilization of "illegal substances." They "use drugs." So, in an effort to "fit in" with this particular peer group, the teenager with low self-esteem will embrace the use of drugs too.

BOREDOM: For the teenager who feels "unloved" by his or her parents, they have no or few "friends," teenage drug use may be a way to escape the boredom of what may seem to be a life without much meaning.

PSYCHOLOGICAL PAIN AND TRAUMA:

If a teenager is being physically abused and or neglected at home, or bullied at school, this will set-them-up for experiencing "psychological trauma."

RESOLUTION OF DRUG ADDICTION ISSUES:

PARENTS AND TEACHERS: The issues involved here will most probably be beyond the ability of the involved teenager to handle or resolve on their own. They (more than likely) will need your support and assistance along with (possibly) professional help to move beyond reliance and dependence on illegal drugs and other narcotic or alcoholic substances.

TEENAGERS READING THIS BOOK: Don't do drugs. Drugs are bad. Drug addiction leads to arrests, poor school performance, difficulty with parents and peer members, dropping out of school, jobless and homelessness.

CHAPTER 20:

BE GOOD TO YOURSELF

This is a very important concept.

What does it mean to "Be Good to Yourself?" Being good to yourself means to love and care enough about yourself that you don't get involved in negative actions or activities: gangs, drug use, or teen pregnancy.

Being good to yourself means that you spend the time in Junior High School, and High School, paying attention to the teachers, coaches and counselors who's job it is to help educate and prepare you for your future.

Put the life lessons and principles detailed in this book to good use.

Be good to yourself.

CHAPTER 21:

GET UP EARLY

Why? Why is it important to get up early? It's because by getting up early, we are getting a head start on the world around us. As children, we are taught the phrase, "the early bird catches the worm." Why? Why is this? It's a simple concept. The bird who awakens first, and starts its day looking for food, is the one who "catches the worm."

Many in the business world, including millionaires and billionaires profess the vital importance of "getting an early start on the day."

Benefits of getting up early:

1. More productivity.

2. Better mental fitness.

3. Better sleep quality.

4. Better test scores.

5. A brighter world-view.

CHAPTER 22:

BE ADAPTABLE

Why? Why is being "adaptable" an important human virtue?

It is because those who can readily, and easily "adapt" to change, new circumstances, obstacles, failures and set-backs, are those who thrive when those who are unable to adapt falter away.

Through the history of human evolution, those who were able to adapt to changing climates, weather patterns, terrain, geography and habitats, were those who survived. Those who were not able to adapt sometimes perished.

Our world is fast moving. Because of ever changing technologies, the advancements coming are ever faster.

As you prepare to leave childhood behind, take one of the most important things a thinking, reasoning, evolving person must have as a necessity: The ability to ADAPT!

EPILOGUE:

Life is a journey; it is a voyage of sorts. The purpose of this book is to help you find your way. It was my intent to share with the young person, the reader, things that may make your journey easier.

If as a young person this book has helped you find a path to success, a path to greater personal growth and development, then I will have done my job as an author, mentor, and guide.

As we say in the United States Navy: Fair Winds, and Following seas.

Good luck to you.